PowerKiDS Readers

AMERICAN SYMBOLS

THE BALD EAGLE

Joe Gaspar

I0808869

PowerKiDS press

New York

Published in 2014 by The Rosen Publishing Group, Inc.
29 East 21st Street, New York, NY 10010

Copyright © 2014 by The Rosen Publishing Group, Inc.

All rights reserved. No part of this book may be reproduced in any form without permission in writing from the publisher, except by a reviewer.

First Edition

Editor: Amelie von Zumbusch
Book Design: Colleen Bialecki

Photo Credits: Cover, pp. 9, 17, 19, 21, 23 iStockphoto/Thinkstock; p. 5 FloridaStock/Shutterstock.com; p. 7 Vladislav Gurfinkel/Shutterstock.com; p. 11 Natalia Lysenko/Shutterstock.com; p. 13 S. R. Maglione/Shutterstock.com; p. 15 Takayuki Maekawa/The Image Bank/Getty Images.

Library of Congress Cataloging-in-Publication Data

Gaspar, Joe.
The bald eagle / by Joe Gaspar. — 1st ed.
p. cm. — (Powerkids readers: American symbols)
Includes index.
ISBN 978-1-4777-0737-1 (library binding) — ISBN 978-1-4777-0815-6 (pbk.) —
ISBN 978-1-4777-0816-3 (6-pack)
1. United States—Seal—Juvenile literature. 2. Bald eagle—United States–Juvenile literature. 3. Emblems, National—United States—Juvenile literature. 4. Animals—Symbolic aspects–Juvenile literature. I. Title.
CD5610.G37 2014
929.90973—dc23

2012043809

Manufactured in the United States of America

CPSIA Compliance Information: Batch #S13PK4: For Further Information contact Rosen Publishing, New York, New York at 1-800-237-9932

CONTENTS

Bald eagles are big.

They are our national bird.

SEAL OF THE PRESIDENT OF THE UNITED STATES
E PLURIBUS UNUM

Fish is their top food.

They live in every state but Hawaii.

They build big nests.

Babies are called **chicks**.

They see well.

"Bald" is an old word for "white."

Their claws are called **talons**.

Have you seen one?

WORDS TO KNOW

bald eagle

chicks

talons

INDEX

WEBSITES

Due to the changing nature of Internet links, PowerKids Press has developed an online list of websites related to the subject of this book. This site is updated regularly. Please use this link to access the list:
www.powerkidslinks.com/pkras/eagle/